Scripture quotations are from The Holy Bible, English Standard Version® (ESV®), copyright © 2001 by Crossway, a publishing ministry of Good News Publishers. Used by permission. All rights reserved.

Photo on page 6 copyright © 2013 Focus on the Family

Photos on pages 10 and 22 copyright © 2013 Cathy Walters

All other photos copyright © 2013 Thinkstock

Concept and Project Director: Derek Hanson

Research and Writing: Glenn T. Stanton, Jim Ware

Editorial Director: Larry Weeden

Why Family Matters

A modern look at an ancient truth

Contents

Foreword

"Why an organization called Focus on the Family that believes so strongly that family matters?" The answer is not as straightforward as you might think. A generation ago, a cultural consensus said that the traditional family was worthy of our support. There was widespread understanding that the nuclear family—a husband and wife committed to each other and devoted to the raising and nurturing of their children—was a powerful force for the common good. Of course, families back then experienced divorce, brokenness, and other trials just as they do today and just as they have throughout recorded history. Nevertheless, in earlier times the traditional family was considered of paramount importance to the well-being of both individuals and society as a whole.

But that is not the case today. The word *family* has all but lost its original meaning in our modern landscape. You don't have to look far to see the fallout. Divorce is the norm. An increasing number of children are growing up in homes where at least one parent is absent. Broken families are the root cause of so many of our social problems, from abuse and addiction to poverty and crime. Our attempts to redefine and reimagine the family only make these problems worse, not better. Somehow, we've lost our way.

And that is where this book comes in. It's designed to

accomplish several things. First, it's an overview of Focus on the Family's mission and values—our very reasons for existence. It's like a guidebook for those of us inside the organization, as well as a primer for those outside, that explains what we do and, more importantly, why it's so critical at this moment in history. Amidst this bleak landscape of familial breakdown, we believe there is reason for *hope*. And that hope comes from the gospel of Jesus Christ and from God's sacred model for the family. His design *works*!

We live in a media-saturated culture that thrives on sound bites but rarely takes the time to dig deeper into the issues. When it comes to the institution of the family, though, we can't afford to skim the surface. We need to have a deep, well-rounded understanding of the family in order to truly grasp its importance. And so another purpose of this book is to serve as a guide for those in the media, giving a fuller-bodied examination of who we are and what we stand for. If we're going to have a conversation about the family, we need to define our terms, and this book is a step in that direction.

Finally, this book serves as an introduction and companion to Focus on the Family's ambitious new initiative called *The Family Project*.™ This program builds on the momentum of *The Truth Project*,® a thirteen-session DVD-based curriculum that outlines the fundamentals of the Christian perspective on life, reality, and the purpose of human existence. The format has been significantly expanded and enhanced for *The Family Project*, encompassing not only a DVD-based curriculum but also a feature-length theatrical documentary titled *Irreplaceable*. The purpose of the documentary and curriculum is to explore what we believe is absolutely essential to a biblical worldview—namely, a deeper understanding of God's design for the family.

Throughout Scripture, God employs the language of *family* to characterize divine relationships. He is repeatedly identified as our heavenly *Father* (Matthew 6:14), and His love for His children is sometimes even equated with that of a *mother* (Luke 13:34). As believers, we are *brothers* [and *sisters*] in Christ (Acts 1:16). And the relationship between Christ and His church is likened to that of a *bridegroom* and his *bride* (Revelation 19:7).

These biblical allusions to the family are not an accident. In a very real sense, they tell us something about almighty God. But they do even more than that. Healthy family dynamics not only reveal the things of God, but they also directly *reflect* Him.

Love. Compassion. Grace. Truth. Self-sacrifice. Thriving families that demonstrate these characteristics in their daily experiences are like signposts pointing toward the Creator of the universe. They give us a glimpse into the heart of God. And they mirror, albeit haltingly and imperfectly, the perfect, holy unity of the Father, the Son, and the Holy Spirit.

"Why focus on the family?" Because the solution to so many of our society's problems can be found in a wholehearted investment in stable, healthy families. In the pages that follow, you'll discover how glimmers of eternal truth flash out to us from the heart of everyday family life.

Jim Daly

President, Focus on the Family

Chapter 1
What Is Family?

This triangle
of truisms,
of father, mother
and child, cannot
be destroyed; it
can only destroy
those civilisations
which disregard it.[1]

G. K. Chesterton

E ach and every one of us came into this world as part of some family. Most of us go on to start families of our own. Like the air we breathe, family is something we can't live without. But family is so natural, so omnipresent, and so fundamental to life that we tend to take it for granted. We assume it will always be there.

That assumption could turn out to be one of the greatest threats facing the world today. For the family, like the earth's natural resources, can be polluted, damaged, or permanently impaired if we don't try to understand what it is, why it is important, and how it can be preserved.

That's the purpose of this little book: to explain, in plain language, what the family is. How did it originate? How does it work? Should and does it have a proper form? And why does it matter for the welfare of men, women, children, communities, our nation, and the world?

Family Is
Fundamental

The first thing we need to understand is that the family is not just some modern, Western, or exclusively Christian idea. It is God's idea.

The family is the natural and inevitable outcome of marriage and parenting. And marriage and parenting, according to the Bible, were the very first assignments that God gave to mankind in the Garden of Eden.

> So God created man in his own image, in the image of God he created him; male and female he created them.
> And God blessed them. And God said to them, "Be fruitful and multiply and fill the earth and subdue it."
>
> Genesis 1:27-28

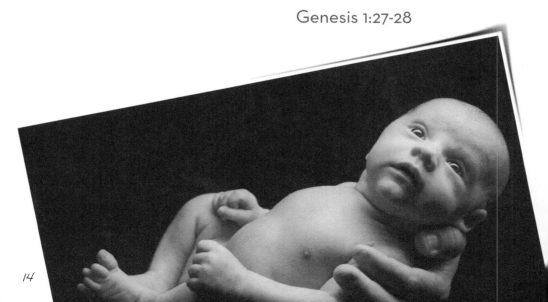

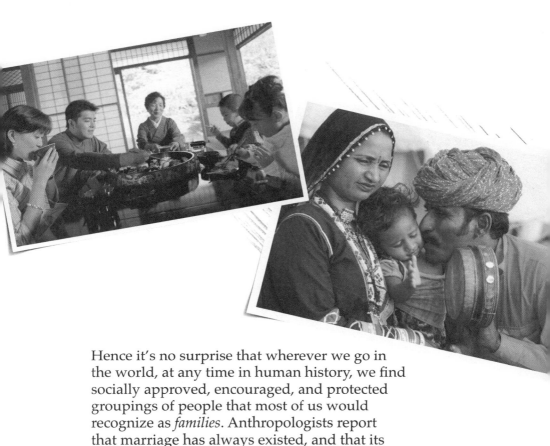

Hence it's no surprise that wherever we go in the world, at any time in human history, we find socially approved, encouraged, and protected groupings of people that most of us would recognize as *families*. Anthropologists report that marriage has always existed, and that its beginnings predate the earliest historical records. Edward Westermarck, one of the most systematic and thorough of those anthropologists who have dedicated themselves to the study of marriage throughout the world's cultures in various ages, explains:

> Marriage . . . is the husband's duty . . . to support his wife and children. . . . That the functions of the husband and father in the family are not merely of the sexual and procreative kind, but involve the duty of protecting the wife and children, is testified by an array of facts relating to peoples in all quarters of the world and in all stages of civilization. . . . As for the origin of the institution of marriage, I consider it probable that it has developed out of a primeval habit.[2]

Almost as if it existed since the creation of the first two people. Of course, the natural attraction between male and female yields results well beyond the sexual embrace. When a baby is born, the woman inevitably finds herself needing to nurture and care for her child. But what about the man? Is there anything in *his* physical makeup that obliges him to stick around and contribute to the well-being of wife and child? Not in his most natural sense. Fatherhood is less natural than motherhood and has to be encouraged by the extended family and the community. This is why the larger community has to make sure there's a durable social mechanism in place that encourages him to do so. That mechanism is the family founded on marriage.

To put it another way, marriage is the way all societies tie men to their children and to the mothers of their children. As anthropologist Margaret Mead said, "When we survey all known human societies, we find everywhere some form of the family, some set of permanent arrangements by which males assist females in caring for children while they are young."[3]

What this tells us is that marriage and family are both *natural*— that is, rooted in creation—and *learned.* In other words, the family is something we need to foster, nurture, and encourage with great care. Even though our physical environment is natural, it still needs to be cared for and protected. The same is true for the human environment founded in family. All cultures at all times must make a purposeful and intentional decision that family matters.

The Cost
of Neglecting the Family

The well-being of the family and the welfare of society go hand in hand. **If we ignore this** connection, there's a high price to be paid for our negligence—a price we can measure in dollars and cents.

A major university study on the fiscal aspects of the problem has revealed that family decline and fragmentation costs U.S. taxpayers more than $112 billion every year, or more than $1 trillion each decade.[4] That's trillion with a "T"! These figures likely understate the actual costs that arise from an increased need for anti-poverty and welfare programs, criminal justice, school nutrition programs, special education, etc.

Beyond economics, unhealthy families result in a tragic loss of benefits to adults, children, and society. (We identify many of these benefits in chapter 4.) Clearly, where the family declines, individuals and communities suffer in significant ways. This has been well-documented in a diversity of reputable research for at least five decades.

Conclusion

Society is composed of individuals whose character is shaped and fostered in the home. That's why those of us at Focus on the Family have committed ourselves over the last three and a half decades to the task of nurturing and defending the family worldwide. Humanity cannot thrive without it.

"Get married? Are you serious?" Tom ridiculed. Raucous laughter exploded from Rob's university buddies around the table. Everyone in the coffee shop looked their direction.

"What's with you guys?" Robert said, gulping his venti mocha. "Don't you think it's about time? Are you guys gonna live in your parents' basement for the next 10 years?"

More laughter shook the cafe, then Tom said, "Marriage is no longer, as they say on campus, a course prerequisite."

After the group broke up, Robert conversed further with a couple of his Christian buddies. One said he wanted to travel the world before getting tied down, and the other expressed worry about being able to support a family without first paying off his student loans and landing a stable job.

Robert had heard that sort of thing before. His ex-fiancée had broken up with him a year ago because she "just wasn't ready," which really meant she wanted to be free and have fun for a while longer, and maybe even prove herself a success in a career before taking on the "burden" of a husband and kids. Besides, Robert had discovered during their engagement that Melissa was actually afraid of any long-term commitments. Her parents, who were Christians, had divorced when she was a freshman. He remembered her tearful words: "If they couldn't make it last a lifetime, who can?"

Weeks later, Robert enrolled in a lab for advanced organic chemistry. The professor paired off the students by last name, so Robert was teamed with a beautiful senior named Hannah. While they juggled test tubes and chemicals, he learned that she was a Christian who had been home-taught all the way through high school, was in line now to be a class valedictorian, and had recruiters from several biotech firms already flooding her in-box with emails.

Way out of my league, Robert thought. But still, they enjoyed working together in the lab, and weeks later when Robert falteringly asked her out for a date, Hannah beamed and said, "I'd love to!" Just like that.

After several months, he proposed to her, and Hannah responded again with an emphatic yes.

"But what about your promising career?" he asked, doubting his good fortune. "The clock is ticking, and starting a family—"

"Being a chemist isn't my top priority right now," Hannah interjected, wrapping her arms around him. "I want you, I want kids, and I want to raise them just like my parents did me. And the sooner the better."

—F. Teller

Chapter 2
The Family
as Part of God's Plan

The Trinity has more often been presented as a dogma to be believed rather than as the living focus of life and thought. . . . In light of the theology of the Trinity, everything looks different.[5]

British theologian Colin E. Gunton

There are lots of pragmatic reasons for helping homes to thrive, and we'll address them in the chapters that follow. But first, can we demonstrate conclusively from Scripture that the family is God's idea? This question needs to be answered before we go any further, since it lays the foundation for everything we do. And the answer is an unequivocal yes.

The Image of
God in Man

How do we know this? The very first chapter of the Bible tells us that family is basic to the meaning of humanity, not only because God created it, but also because He meant it to reflect His image in creation. Mankind was made to be a *picture* of God—a visible, tangible, understandable representation of who He is and what He is like. In humanity, the invisible God mysteriously becomes visible. And that's not all. Genesis 1:27 teaches us plainly that mankind fulfills this role by being both male and female. The first humans were created as a couple, and it's precisely as man and woman together that they mirror God's very nature.

The Trinity

In chapter 1 we noted that the family arises naturally out of this coming together of male and female. The union of the sexes within the bond of marriage produces children, thus fulfilling God's commandment to "be fruitful and multiply" (Genesis 1:28). So far, so good. Now let's see if we can discover why this process is so important from a biblical point of view.

God had something very special in mind when He created Eve and brought her to Adam. As the Bible puts it,

> Then the LORD God said, "It is not good that the man should be alone; I will make him a helper fit for him."
>
> Genesis 2:18

Why was it not good for the man to be alone? First, God saw that Adam needed a helper, a companion. But there's more to it than that. By himself, Adam could not reflect "the image of God," because as the Bible tells us, God is *love* (1 John 4:8, emphasis added), and love can happen only between two or more persons. So then, it's primarily as *lover and beloved* in a relationship of mutual give-and-take that Adam and Eve reveal the nature of God. God is himself a community of three divine Persons living together and loving one another within the unity of the Godhead.

Now, the story doesn't end there. For Adam and Eve reflect

this beautiful and mysterious relational nature even more perfectly when, through becoming "one flesh" (Genesis 2:24), they participate with God in creating a third and distinct person (4:1)—in other words, when they beget and bear children. So it's through the *family*—this new human community of husband, wife, and child—that mankind most clearly shows forth the trinitarian nature of God.

There is, of course, an infinite difference between the eternal mystery of love and creativity within the Trinity and the physical manner in which male and female generate new life in the human family. After all, God is spirit, not flesh. Nevertheless, in the biblical vision, human sexuality reflects something—or is *intended* to reflect something—of the eternal exchange of life-giving love found in

the Holy Trinity. As theologian Michael Downey puts it in his book *Altogether Gift,*

> The human person is not an individual, not a self-contained being who at some stage in life chooses or elects to be in relationship with another and others. . . . From our origin we are related to others. We are from others, by others, toward others, for others, just as it is in God to exist in the relations of interpersonal love.[6]

The doctrine of the Trinity teaches us that the core of the universe consists of love, intimacy, and community. God is fundamentally personal and relational. As His image-bearers, we reflect this grand nature. And we do it most effectively in community, starting with the family: the fundamental human "trinity" (with a small "t") of husband, wife, and child—literally one flesh, three human persons.

The Final
Consummation

We've seen that the Bible begins with a wedding. Significantly, it also ends with one. The book of Genesis documented the marriage of the first man and woman, Adam and Eve. The final chapters of Revelation celebrate a wedding of a very different kind: the marriage of Christ and His redeemed and beautiful bride, the church:

> Then I heard what seemed to be the voice of a great multitude, like the roar of many waters and like the sound of mighty peals of thunder, crying out,
> "Hallelujah!
> For the Lord our God the Almighty reigns.
> Let us rejoice and exult and give him the glory, for the marriage of the Lamb has come, and his Bride has made herself ready; it was granted her to clothe herself with fine linen, bright and pure"—for the fine linen is the righteous deeds of the saints.
> And the angel said to me, "Write this: Blessed are those who are invited to the marriage supper of the Lamb." And he said to me, "These are the true words of God."
> Revelation 19:6-9 (see also 21:9; 22:17)

This is not just sentimental imagery. It speaks deeply and beautifully of the nature of God, the destiny of His people, and just how important marriage and family are within the scheme of God's grand and overarching plan. For when Jesus says that in the culmination of time we will not give or be given in marriage (Matthew 22:30), it is not because marriage is somehow second-

rate. It is because the *meaning* of marriage will be gloriously fulfilled at the wedding of the Lamb.

As the apostle Paul said, " 'Therefore a man shall leave his father and mother and hold fast to his wife, and the two shall become one flesh.' This mystery is profound, and I am saying that it refers to Christ and the church" (Ephesians 5:31-32). Since we *are* the church, we will live eternally as Christ's bride. Isn't this a beautiful and hopeful truth?

Potential
Misunderstandings

B efore closing this chapter, let's admit that some verses in the New Testament might leave readers feeling confused about God's view of the family. For example, Jesus said, "If anyone comes to me and does not *hate* his own father and mother and wife and children and brothers and sisters, yes, and even his own life, he cannot be my disciple" (Luke 14:26, emphasis added). And in Matthew 12:49-50, when informed that His mother and brothers were looking for Him, Christ seemed to dismiss the value of blood relationships in this way: "Stretching out his hand toward his disciples, he said, 'Here are my mother and my brothers! For whoever does the will of my Father in heaven is my brother and sister and mother.' "

Does this suggest that Jesus, like some modern advocates of social re-engineering, considered the family to be passé? Was He saying, in effect, that the church has rendered the family irrelevant? Not in the least. If we look at these statements in context—as well as in the larger story that the Scriptures are telling us—we can see that they actually give the family a place of honor.

Jesus never said that family isn't important to God. What He *did* say is that a disciple's love for Him should be so great and so overpowering that it eclipses all other loves. Even the strongest and most compelling of our natural human loves ought to look like "hate" when compared with our love for Christ. We should be so fully committed to Him that we would be willing to give up even the very *best* things in life if called upon to do so. And family *is* one of the very best and most important things in life.

That's the whole point. Jesus himself remained in His own family. His mom was there and involved in His first miracle. And she was at His crucifixion, with Jesus even commanding John to care for her in His absence. While the Savior was on the cross, He was thinking of His mother. He certainly did not forsake His family. He was mindful of it right up to the end of His earthly life.

Conclusion

Family, then, is integral not only to *human* nature, but also to God's *own* nature. From the first page of Scripture to the last, we are reminded again and again that, this side of heaven, marriage and the family is the best and most accurate representation we have of the intimate, relational, and loving character of the triune God. This is our biblical and theological reason for our conviction that family matters.

In spite of exhaustion and a nagging cold, Mark managed to make it to his church's weekend men's conference. Late Saturday night, Stan, a man Mark respected, approached him.

"Can I be honest with you?" Stan asked.

"Sure," Mark replied.

"Mark," he said, "I see you as a guy who's strung out. You want to do everything well, and you're trying to do everything. But you can't; you'll burn out. How many hours per week do you work?"

"Probably 55 to 65," Mark replied.

"You need to cut it to 40," Stan said.

"Stan," Mark protested, "I don't know anyone who works 40 hours."

Stan, who owned his own company, replied, "Well, I don't know anyone who *doesn't* work 40. You just make it happen. Has Shelly ever talked to you about this?"

"Yeah, of course."

"Don't wait until you're as old as I am to listen to your wife," Stan said. "God gives us our wives for a reason."

Later Mark reflected, "When he had that conversation with me, it snapped me to attention. There were a few things converging in my life: that conversation, talking with Shelly back at home, and a sermon I heard called 'Choosing to Cheat' by Andy Stanley, which pointed out our lack of time to get everything done that we want. All of us have to 'cheat' someone out of the time we'd like to spend on them, and we tend to give our best to work or our hobbies, and cheat our family, who gets the leftovers."

Even after Mark and Shelly decided he would cut back,

Mark didn't know if he could pull it off. "I had just turned in an aggressive budget for my work," he said. "If you're working 60 hours and you suddenly cut back to 40, you're essentially cutting a part-time person from your office. But Stan pep-talked me enough, and Shelly and I followed through with the decision. In the end, we believed he was right."[7]

—Dr. Kevin Leman

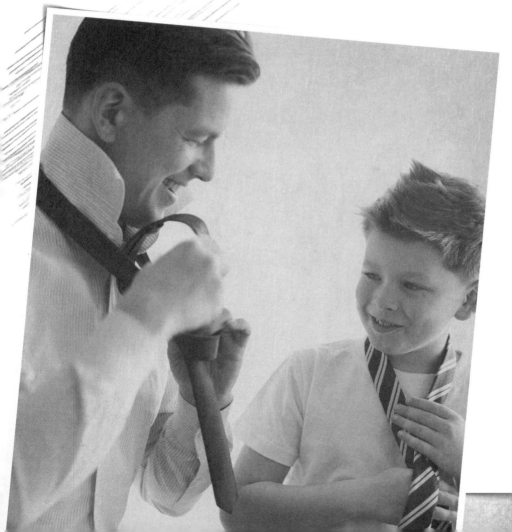

Chapter 3

What Makes a Healthy Family?

All happy families

resemble one another,

each unhappy family is unhappy

in its own way.

Leo Tolstoy,
Anna Karenina

The Bible tells us that God is not the author of chaos and confusion, but of harmony, order, and peace (1 Corinthians 14:33). Since the family is God's idea, it follows that He must have had an orderly plan in mind when He created it: a pattern or template defining, in a clear and balanced way, what His idea of family should look like.

Does such a pattern or template exist? We think so. That's why we're confident that something can be done to help families thrive.

No Perfect Families

If we agree that God has an ideal plan for the family, the next thing we need to realize is that nobody lives up to it. *There are no perfect families*. This should be obvious, especially to anyone who knows biblical history. From Adam and Eve to Cain and Abel, from Abraham and Sarah to Lot and his daughters, from Jacob and Esau to David and Bathsheba, Scripture shows us plainly that even the most storied families have "issues."[8] To be human is to be flawed.

The Bible also tells us why this is true. When God created the world, He made everything good (Genesis 1:31). Unfortunately, that goodness was compromised when mankind rebelled and fell into sin. Since the Fall, nothing has been precisely as God intended it to be. Creation has been out of whack ever since Adam and Eve made the fatal decision to disobey God.

Because of their choice, the world now exists in an abnormal state. In the physical realm, this abnormality shows up in the form of thorns, thistles, pains, pangs, and the hardship of man's daily struggle for survival (see Genesis 3:17-19; Romans 8:20-23). In family life, it takes the shape of conflict, broken relationships, and an inability to give and receive love.

Getting Back
on Track

Does this mean that the family is in a hopeless situation? Thankfully not. The gospel is all about redemption. As Christians, we believe that the Lord is in the business of fixing broken things. He heals the sick, raises the dead, seeks the lost, and restores the dispossessed to their rightful place. Through faith in His saving power, even the most dismally fragmented family can be made whole.

And that's not all. Even among the unredeemed, the principles that God built into His original design remain operative. That's why an unbelieving family might sometimes be happier, healthier, and better adjusted than a particular family inside the church. They're happier and healthier because, whether they realize it or not, their family conforms to aspects of God's blueprint or plan.

*There are
no perfect families.*
This should be obvious
to anyone who knows
biblical history.

Qualities of
a Healthy Marriage and Family

I s it possible to get a handle on that plan? Can we distill God's standard for the family into simpler, comprehensible language and use it in everyday life to make families stronger and better? Once again, we think the answer is yes. And it's precisely at this point that we can benefit from the observations of those who have adopted a scientific approach to the study of the family.

We've examined all the best research and come up with a list of qualities that seem to characterize successful families. Interestingly enough, most of the studies we used were not conducted by Christian scholars, nor did they seek to determine what makes a healthy *Christian* family. Instead, these findings come from sociologists and psychologists who have observed smoothly functioning marriages and families in a variety of cultural settings around the world.[9] Here are seven of the most important qualities they identified:

1 **Big picture:** Scholars say successful families realize that the meaning of family is bigger than themselves. We, of course, believe that the family comes from God and exists for God as well as the larger community. This helps us see our families and those around us in the proper, larger perspective.

2 **Commitment:** Thriving families are committed to the long haul in marriage and parenting. They make family a top priority, putting it above their personal wants and desires. They know that love is more than just an emotion.

3 **High regard:** A healthy family demonstrates mutual respect, honor, care, and concern for all family members. It emphasizes affirmation and encouragement and downplays criticism.

4 **Flexibility and grace:** No family can survive if its members are not willing to bend and flex with one another. Grace, forgiveness, and a sense of safety are absolutely essential to smoothly functioning family relationships.

5 **Balance:** Balanced parents expect obedience from their children, but they also encourage individuality. They realize that love, and not rigid adherence to rules, is the key to healthy human development.

6 **Joy and humor:** Thriving families intentionally create an atmosphere of joy. They laugh together, play together, and delight in one another. But they avoid making jokes at someone's expense.

7 **A service mindset:** Finally, happy, balanced families care about the world around them. They take seriously the idea that the world will be a poorer place if they don't do their part to serve others.

Essential Behaviors
for Parents and Kids

Are some families just destined to exhibit those seven qualities while others are not? Is family success a matter of luck? Or are there certain things you and your family can do to foster healthy growth in these key areas? We believe there are. Here's a list of a dozen behaviors that, when pursued, will get you moving in the right direction. They are as powerful as they are simple.

1

Pray together: A high regard for prayer should begin with Mom and Dad. Couples who pray together stay together; research demonstrates this to be true. Parents also show their kids by example what it means to rely on God for all of life's daily concerns.

2

Participate in a local church together: Couples strengthen their commitment to one another—and families grow in a sense of unity—when they form meaningful relationships with members of God's larger family and together hear God's Word proclaimed each week in worship. No Christian should be a free agent or lone ranger.

3 Perform daily acts of kindness: Small, sacrificial words and deeds draw spouses closer together and create a positive environment for the growth and development of healthy, balanced kids.

4 Learn your spouse's love language: Ask your spouse from time to time, "How can I love you better this week?" Show your love in ways that he or she will understand. Set a good example for your kids by demonstrating affection for one another and engaging in mutual acts of kindness and service.

5 Eat dinner together: Do this at least four nights a week. Research consistently shows that the family that shares meals together not only stays together but actually enjoys it. Don't allow anything—phone, television, or text messages—to interrupt these rituals of family togetherness and communion.

6 Be actively involved in your children's education: Join in their school activities. Know their teachers and the subjects they're studying. Checking their homework every night makes a big difference. Beyond boosting their academic achievement, this encourages parent-child interaction. It also tells your child that he or she is worth your time.

7 Know your kids' friends, and know where they are: Accountability is essential for healthy families. Insist that your children let you know where they are, whom they are with, and what they are doing. This will show them that you love them and care about them.

Get inside their world: Make a point of reading the books your kids are reading, listening to their favorite music, and watching movies or television programs with them. If you do this, you'll be in a much better position to exert a positive influence over their cultural tastes and to discuss with them intelligently the pros and cons of the entertainment choices they're making.

8

Give the benefit of the doubt: In family life, positive sentiments should always override the negative. Whether in parenting or in your marital relationship, never choose to think the worst of the other person when something goes wrong. No relationship can stand on such a foundation. Expect the best and be willing to overlook mistakes and faults as an expression of love and grace.

9

10 Play together: Something wonderful happens when children and parents get down on the floor to play together, when they enjoy board games or outdoor activities as a family, or when they learn to play instruments and make music together. Don't miss these opportunities to strengthen family ties.

11 Give praise and show love: Husbands need respect. Wives long to know that they are cared for and loved. Children need the security that can only be provided by caring moms and dads. Create a home where all these needs are met, and you will have a healthy, thriving family.

12 Lasting faith: Some of the best research shows that ensuring our children enter their adult years with a vibrant, enduring faith is not as complex as we might think.[10] The biggest factor is making sure they live in a family that practices their faith regularly and seriously. You certainly don't have to be perfect, but just diligent disciples of Jesus. Children who learn that Bible reading, prayer, and regular worship are important and practice these are likely to continue to do so in their later years. Also, having other adults around them who take their faith seriously—extended family, teachers, coaches, family friends—has a strong impact. Children who have these are likely to keep a lifelong and growing faith.

These behaviors are not difficult to understand, nor are they the prerogative of the wealthy or highly educated. They're available to everyone. Practicing them consistently will not necessarily solve all your family's problems, but you will begin to grow in grace, love, happiness, health, and relational durability.

And that's important, because your healthy, happy family is something the world desperately needs.

My work with the Juvenile Justice Ministry of Metro Chicago Youth for Christ puts me in constant contact with kids on the street, gangbangers, and young drug dealers. After 50 years on the bricks, I'm not easily shocked, but this particular morning I had to sit down as I read, "Shavon Dean, killed Sunday, was 14. Her suspected killer, Robert ('Yummy') Sandifer, was 11. Those charged in his slaying are 16 and 14."

Three families had been sucked into a terrible tragedy. I shook my head sadly. I'd attended too many of these funerals, with grieving families crying, "Why? Why?"

Gradually I pieced together what could be known from the in-depth media reporting.

Sunday, August 18, 10:30 a.m.

Robert Sandifer, known to family and friends as Yummy because of his love of cookies and candy, left his grandmother's house to go hang out with friends. The woman who had helped raise Yummy may have suspected her grandson was spending time with the Black Disciples gang, but as with most parents and grandparents, denial came easily. Robert wasn't in a gang. Not her Yummy. Why, he was only 11, a child.

Sunday, August 18, 9:00 p.m.

Shavon Dean's mother was grilling ribs and chicken in back of the family dwelling when the 14-year-old girl left the house to walk a friend home. As the girls passed a group of boys playing football, a burst of gunfire shattered the calm. Shavon Dean was found lying on the ground, a bullet in her head. When the police arrived, the frantic witnesses all agreed: Yummy Sandifer had walked up to the group and opened fire with a 9-mm semiautomatic pistol.

Monday and Tuesday, August 19–20

The police initiated a massive manhunt for one vicious boy who, for reasons unknown, had gone on a shooting spree. Some people weren't surprised when they heard Yummy was the suspect. His mother was a crack addict, and his father was in jail. The boy had been abused, neglected, and in and out of "the system" for numerous felonies since he was three years old.

Thursday, August 29

A news bulletin flashed on TV. Passersby had seen the body of a young boy, soon identified as Yummy, lying in a pool of blood in a pedestrian tunnel under a train viaduct at 108th and Dauphin. He'd been shot twice in the back of the head.[11]

—Gordon McLean

Chapter 4
Why Healthy Families Matter

The business done in the home is nothing less than the shaping of the bodies and souls of humanity. The family is the factory that manufactures mankind.[12]

G. K. Chesterton

So far we've argued that the family is God's idea, that God created it with an ideal plan or pattern in mind, and that families conforming to this pattern are, on the whole, healthier and happier.

But what about the individual members of a good family? Are they better off? And what about society in general? Is there any evidence that thriving families have a positive impact on the larger community?

In this chapter we want to show that good marriages and families are beneficial for everyone. They're good for individuals, both inside and outside the family structure. They're also good for society as a whole. Let's take a closer look at why and how this is so.

Benefits to the Individual: *Adults*

In chapter 1, we said that marriage and family go together. They are two sides of the same coin. That's worth remembering here, because when we talk about the benefits of family life for individual adults, we're really talking about the benefits of marriage. As it turns out, the social and psychological sciences have a great deal to say on this subject. Here are some of their most striking findings.

Physical health and longevity. Old bachelors like to joke about marriage being a "ball and chain." It's all downhill after the wedding, they say. But the opposite is true. University of Chicago sociologist Linda Waite, in her book *The Case for Marriage*, states, "The evidence from four decades of research is surprisingly clear: a good marriage is both men's and women's best bet for living a long and healthy life."[13] Dr. Robert Coombs of UCLA finds "an intimate link between marital status and personal well-being." He adds, "Virtually every study of mortality and marital status shows the unmarried of both sexes have higher death rates, whether by accident, disease, or self-inflicted wounds, and this is found in every country that maintains accurate health statistics."[14]

Happiness. A number of studies have found that marriage tends to be related to elevated levels of personal happiness. A recent study involving 17 industrialized nations with diverse social and institutional frameworks found a dramatic connection between marital status and happiness:

> "BEING MARRIED WAS **3.4** times more closely tied to the variance in happiness than was cohabitation, and marriage increases happiness equally among men and women. . . . Further, the strength of the association between being married and being happy is remarkably consistent across nations."[15]

Mental health. Marriage also elevates one's sense of happiness and contentment. Professor Susan Brown, writing in the *Journal of Health and Social Behavior*, tells us that "marital status is a key determinant of psychological well-being."[16] Researchers at Yale University and UCLA make a similar assertion: "One of the most consistent findings in psychiatric epidemiology is that married persons enjoy better . . . health than the unmarried."[17] Other scholars working with data from the United States and the United Kingdom estimate "the size of the marriage effect upon mental well-being to be equal to that from an extra 100,000 dollars a year."[18] That's valuable mental health.

> This and other research shows these mental health benefits actually decline in important ways among cohabiters. In other words, it's not just sharing life with a "significant other" that makes the difference. It's a particular type of relationship that confers these mental health benefits: **marriage**.

Finances. Married men and women tend to earn more, save more, and use their money more strategically than the unmarried. Compared to individuals with intact first marriages, those who have never married see a 75 percent reduction in overall wealth, while those who cohabit experience a 58 percent reduction. Those who divorce and don't remarry have an overall wealth reduction of 72 percent.[19] Why? According to Berkeley's George Akerlof, a Nobel Prize–winning labor economist, it's because "the job performance of married employees appears to be significantly better than the job performance of single employees."[20] Married workers have a stronger motivation to work hard and stick with their jobs, which is why they typically get promoted more quickly, get fired less frequently, and miss fewer days of work.

Sex. Contrary to Hollywood stereotypes, the people who report the highest levels of sexual satisfaction are not carefree, swinging singles. On the contrary, they're faithfully married couples who entered marriage as virgins. "In real life," says a study conducted by sociologists from the University of

Chicago, "the unheralded, seldom discussed world of married sex is actually the one that satisfies people the most."[21] Moreover, married couples who have a sincere faith and who pray together regularly tend to have a more fulfilling sex life than the general married population.[22]

Benefits to the Individual: *Children*

Child Trends, a non-partisan child advocacy organization based in Washington, DC, examined how family structure affects children.

> An extensive body of research tells us that children do best when they grow up with both biological parents in a low-conflict marriage. . . . Thus, it is not simply the presence of two parents, as some have assumed, but the presence of two [married] biological parents that seems to support children's development.[23]

Exactly how are these kids better off than their counterparts who don't live with their own parents? Let's look at five key indicators.

1. Infant mortality.

Infants of all races who are conceived by unmarried women are much more likely to die at or near birth, to have low birth weights, or to be born prematurely. According to the journal *Social Science and Medicine*, the babies of unwed *white* mothers over the age of twenty are surprisingly at greater risk of dying in infancy than those of other races.[24] This is true even in countries with nationalized health care systems and strong support systems for single mothers.[25]

2. Child mental health.

The National Center for Health Statistics says that children living with their own married parents require professional attention for psychological problems at *half* the rate of those belonging to single, divorced, or cohabiting households.[26] Judith Wallerstein, a scholar who has conducted some of the most extensive studies in this area, contends that serious emotional and relational difficulties follow children of divorce throughout adolescence and actually tend to grow worse as they enter adulthood.[27] Princeton's celebrated sociologist of the family, Sara McLanahan, finds this may be due in part to the absence of fathers through the breakup of families or fathers never being on the scene.[28] The *Review of General Psychology* agrees: "Overall, father love appears to be as heavily implicated as mother love in offsprings' psychological well-being and health."[29]

3. Poverty. Prior to the 1940s, parental unemployment was the primary cause of family poverty. From the fifties to the seventies it was lack of education. Since then, poverty has been more closely correlated with family structure. Isabel Sawhill, a scholar with the Brookings Institution, agrees. In her view, "the proliferation of single-parent households accounts for virtually all of the increase in child poverty since the early 1970s."[30] Similarly, W. Bradford Wilcox and his team of leading family scholars tell us that "when parents fail to marry and stay married, children are more likely to experience deep and persistent poverty, even after controlling for race and family background."[31]

4. Education. The famous 1966 Coleman Report on education, called *Equality of Educational Opportunity*, concluded that the leading contributor to academic achievement among school children was the family and a sound family structure.[32] Data gathered since that time has only strengthened that conclusion. Children living with their two married biological or adoptive parents consistently earn the highest grades, while children living with their mother and an unmarried partner receive the lowest grades.[33] On average, children from married, intact families have higher test scores and grade point averages, less absenteeism, and greater expectations of attending college than children living with one parent.[34] Additionally, among children who attend college, those from married, two-parent families are 7 to 20 percent more likely to finish.[35]

> Dr. Susan Brown has determined that marriage, not just the presence of biological parents, has the greatest effect upon a child's educational success. Children living with cohabiting parents show outcomes that are similar to their peers from single-parent homes.[36]

5. Family stability. Family break-up has serious and long-term emotional, physical, financial, and behavioral consequences for children *and* adults.[37] But which families tend to break up the most? Professor Wendy Manning, writing in the *Population Research and Policy Review*, says children with cohabiting parents are 292 percent more likely to see their parents break up, compared to their peers with married parents. If these cohabiting parents do eventually marry, the risk of disruption is still 151 percent greater than for children born to married-only parents.[38]

> This increased risk of family dissolution also affects the growing number of children who are being raised by same-sex parents. The National Longitudinal Lesbian Family Study found that lesbian households break up at a much higher rate than heterosexual families (56 percent versus 36 percent).[39] But this study lumped cohabiting heterosexual and married heterosexual homes together, and as we saw above, cohabiters break up at high rates. So we have to conclude from this study that lesbian-headed homes are *dramatically* more likely to break up compared with married, mother-father homes. Other studies have similar findings.[40]

Benefits to *Society*

We've already established that the family is the basic building block of human society. The larger community is composed of individuals whose character is shaped and fostered in the home. As goes the family, so goes the entire culture. That's why the family is not just a "social construct" or "private" arrangement. On the contrary, its health and well-being are matters of grave public concern.

Strong families benefit the nation and the entire world in a number of important ways. Where should we look if we want to see this principle played out in everyday life? Here again, empirical research can point us in the right direction. It corroborates biblical wisdom in some striking ways. Let's examine a few areas.

Poverty. We've already noted that marriage tends to be a wealth-building institution, and that children who grow up in two-parent homes are far less likely to experience poverty at any stage of life. Here we simply need to add that this aspect of marriage and family life has implications not only for the individuals concerned, but also for our entire economic system. "Compared with those raised by single parents," write the authors of *The Future of the Family*, "children raised by both biological parents earn more in the labor market, are less likely to be poor, have more assets, and are in a better position to insure themselves against economic uncertainties."[41] It should be obvious that this benefits everybody.

Crime. Crime goes up when the health of the family goes down. After taking important socio-economic factors into account, boys from single-parent homes are about twice as likely to commit a crime leading to incarceration by age thirty as their peers who were raised in married homes. Those from stepfamilies are "more than two and a half times as likely"![42] No wonder research from Stanford University concludes that "such family measures as the percentage of the population divorced, the percentage of households headed by women, and the percentage of unattached individuals in the community are among the most powerful predictors of crime rates."[43]

Sexual dysfunction. As we've seen, married couples generally prove to be the most sexually satisfied adults in the entire population, which suggests that marriage cuts down on the amount of sexual dissatisfaction and dysfunction in society. This, in turn, translates into a happier, healthier, and safer environment for everyone. Individuals who are sexually maladjusted usually don't make good neighbors, teachers, coaches, or citizens.

The absence of fathers. A father is not just a second parent or a reliable provider. A father is a different kind of parent, and his children benefit in many ways from his distinctive influence. All the relevant research demonstrates that high levels of father involvement dramatically boost every important measure of child well-being.[44] That's why every presidential administration for the last 20 years has taken steps to promote dads' involvement in the lives of their kids.

Domestic violence. Research reveals a close correlation between marital status and domestic violence. But this connection is different from what some people might expect. On the whole, it isn't wives who are suffering at the hands of their husbands, or children who are being abused by their own married parents. On the contrary, the kids most threatened by physical, sexual, and verbal abuse are those who share quarters with Mom and her live-in boyfriend.[45] Also, a woman with a wedding ring on her finger is more than three times *less* likely to become the victim of any form of abuse than women who are single, cohabiting, or divorced.[46] That's because marriage actually tends to foster greater respect for women; it's a feminist institution in the best sense.

Substance abuse. Government reports on the relationship between adolescent drug use and family structure indicate that, regardless of gender, age, family income, race, or ethnicity, kids who don't live with their own married mother and father are between 50 and 150 percent more likely to abuse drugs than those being raised in intact families.[47] The breakup of the family is good news only for pushers.

The Social Cost of *Family Failure*

In chapter 1 we noted that the demise of healthy marriages and intact families is very costly. Money isn't everything, of course—not by a long shot. But it *can* serve as a strong indicator of the correlation between family well-being and the vitality of our communities, states, and nation.

When marriage is neglected and families dissolve, **everyone** pays the price. **Especially** our children.

A staggering proportion of the tax dollars paid by Americans to fund social service systems—programs such as housing assistance, food stamps, child welfare, and crime prevention—has been necessitated by the breakup of the family. Clearly, it *does* matter how people choose to live their lives. When marriage is neglected and families dissolve, everyone pays the price. Especially our children.

Conclusion

All of this has an important bearing on a subject that's being hotly debated in the public square today. Should society have anything to say about marriage? Should government level the playing field and treat all intimate relationships as equal? Is the question of whom you love and whom you choose to live with a purely private and personal matter, or does it have profound and wide-ranging societal ramifications?

Based on the evidence we've presented in this chapter—evidence drawn from objective, empirical science—we have to conclude that marriage and family are about something much bigger than a man, a woman, and the children produced by their union. Among many, it is really about—quite literally—the love of neighbor, because strong families are high on the list of things that enhance human well-being. It should be plain to anyone who examines the facts that marriage and family are public institutions and that it's in the best interests of the entire human community to protect and encourage them so they survive and thrive. Leading sociologist James Q. Wilson humorously commented, "The evidence as to the powerful effect of this familial foundation is now so strong that even some sociologists believe it."[48]

Through her tears, Julia looked at Pete and said, "Do you *ever* plan on telling people we're engaged?"

"Julia," he began slowly, "I just can't go through with this. I wouldn't treat you fairly. It's not right." Back when he'd proposed to Julia, his intentions had been honorable; now he was feeling more and more nervous about marrying her. It was no secret that his wealthy and powerful social circle didn't approve of her. To his parents and to his friends, she was only a poor, uneducated girl who had captured Pete with her beauty.

Julia was devastated by their broken engagement. For months she tried to move on with her life. Then one day Pete called to say, "Julia, I can't stand living without you. I'm totally falling apart. You've *got* to marry me." Against her better judgment, she eventually consented, and they were married. In a few years, the Flannerys had three children, settled into their dream home, and began attending a growing church. Finally their life together seemed to be getting more comfortable. But their tumultuous history had left a deep imprint on Julia; she still felt unappreciated, unworthy, and insecure.

Pete and Julia began doing things with some new neighbors, Rolf and Lisa Hartman. The couples even attended the same church. As the friendship progressed, Julia realized she had more in common with Rolf than anyone else. On the tennis court, she and Rolf played against Pete and Lisa.

"We won!" Julia exclaimed one day, running over to high-five Rolf.

Rolf draped his arm around her shoulders as they walked to the net to shake hands with Pete and Lisa. "Nice shot!" he said warmly, squeezing Julia's arm. Then he flashed his blinding-white smile at her. Julia inhaled sharply.

Weeks later, after another tennis match, Rolf leaned close to Julia and whispered, "I heard Pete's going out of town next weekend on Valentine's Day. Maybe I'll stop by." Julia was shocked and told herself she didn't want anything to happen. After all, she was a Christian and a married woman. Still, she found it flattering that someone as successful and handsome as Rolf might find her attractive.

You can guess the rest. The affair that ensued went on for months, with Julia often making half-hearted attempts to break it off. She felt so guilty for hurting Pete in this way. Pete soon suspected the affair, but he was determined to win back his wife's love. He gave her the attention and love she'd craved for so long. He listened to her and asked her opinions. He told her she was beautiful and that he loved her. That made Julia feel even more guilty.

Eventually, through counseling and the intervention of concerned Christians, the affair ended. Pete forgave Julia, and the two of them went to Santa Fe, New Mexico, for a two-day marriage retreat. There a therapist addressed topics that helped the Flannerys understand why their marriage had been vulnerable to an affair. Pete saw not only how his past words and actions had made Julia feel inadequate, but also how his lack of affection had hurt her. She needed to be held and loved, to be given more attention. Julia saw how she could improve her communication skills as well.

"Nothing is as wonderful as beginning to live a life of integrity," she later told Pete. "I'm so thankful you stuck by me through this."

Pete smiled and took her hand. "We're going to make it," he said.[49]

—Betsy Holt and Mike Yorkey

Chapter 5
Problems Facing Families Today

It can rightly
be said that
marriage
and the family
are institutions
under siege
in our world
today, and that
with marriage
and the family,
our very
civilization
is in crisis.[50]

Andreas J. Kostenberger
and David W. Jones,
God, Marriage, and Family

We've admitted that there are no perfect families. In our fallen world, none of us can measure up to the standard that God had in mind when He created human beings in His image and commanded man and woman to "be fruitful and multiply." But we've also seen that the family is not without hope. Even though our families can't be perfect, that's no excuse for neglecting them or allowing them to fall apart. On the contrary, our assignment is to make them the best they can possibly be.

The Bible calls us to this task over and over again. The emphasis in the Scriptures on the value of marriage and the family shows up right away in the creation account (Genesis 1:27-28; 2:23-24). It resurfaces in Deuteronomy 11:19 and Proverbs 22:6, where the Lord instructs His people to train their children in the way of holiness and truth. It's behind the psalmist's declaration that "children are a heritage from the LORD, the fruit of the womb a reward" (Psalm 127:3) and the apostle Paul's solemn warning that "if anyone does not provide for his relatives, and especially for members of his household, he has denied the faith and is worse than an unbeliever" (1 Timothy 5:8). Clearly, there is a strong and inescapable biblical basis for emphasizing the family. God wants us to work hard at helping our families thrive.

Unfortunately, this isn't easy. It never has been easy, for the simple reason that people have always been sinful, and Satan directs many of his strongest attacks against the family precisely because of what it represents. But fostering family life is especially difficult today. Why? Because the family is under pressure as never before. It's facing a number of daunting obstacles that are unique to the modern age, both at home and in the culture. Let's identify some of these issues.

Individual Family Issues

The pace of modern life, the practical implications of technological advancement, changes in social attitudes due to major cultural shifts—these and many other factors have combined in subtle and not-so-subtle ways to undermine the quality of family relationships today. Here's how they play out on a practical level.

Insufficient time. It's been said that success in family life is spelled T-I-M-E. Apart from love itself, nothing is more crucial to the health and well-being of a thriving family. Unfortunately, few commodities are in shorter supply today. Nobody, it seems, has enough hours to do everything that needs to be done even though we are each allotted the same 24 hours in each day. Thus, it becomes singly a matter of priority. And no one suffers more under these circumstances than children. Kids need lots of time with Mom and Dad if they're to develop into healthy, well-adjusted adults. They need this more than afternoons and weekends full of activities and sports, which too many parents confuse with good parenting. Too often, it is not.

Meaningful parent-child interaction can't be scheduled like a business meeting. It has to unfold naturally as mothers, fathers, and kids spend quantities of time together in a relaxed and unstructured setting.

Busyness. Time is short because people are busy. That includes parents and children. Mothers and fathers desperately need to learn what it means to put family ahead of career and other personal achievements. They also need to free themselves from the notion that a full schedule of activities for the kids is a sign of good parenting.

Lack of vision. Today we are perhaps more confused about the family than any other generation in the last few centuries. We are not as clear as we should be on the nature of the family, and we are being constantly challenged by various competing views. But we must hold and teach a vision for what the family is and can be. We must understand the shared purpose that God may have in mind for the members of our own households and those of our extended family, friends, and neighbors. Without this larger vision, we all find it harder to work together and stay committed to one another when times get tough.

Individualism. Whether they realize it or not, many of our contemporaries are focusing their energy on looking out for No. 1. As a result, they tend to view marriage and family as nothing more than a means of achieving individual happiness. This is the opposite of the way it's supposed to work. In the Christian view, personal fulfillment is a by-product of service to others.

Isolation. Isolation and alienation are traits of the modern age. Generally speaking, families today don't have the strong connections with a larger community that were part of the fabric of life in past generations. Christian families need to remember that God has called them to be part of the body of Christ and that the church is meant to function as a *family of families*. This means developing significant relationships with other believers, not just "attending" church.

Deficiencies in parenting skills and attitudes. Good parenting requires understanding, patience, direction, wisdom, and perseverance. This isn't rocket science, but neither is it always intuitive. Family life is deteriorating today in part because many moms and dads don't put as much intentional thought and effort into raising their children as they do for their jobs, hobbies, and other personal interests.

Bitterness and anger. Anger is a natural human response to disappointment or unfair treatment. But anger that isn't acknowledged and dealt with (Ephesians 4:26) can become a root of bitterness in the heart (Hebrews 12:15). Bitterness poisons the soul of the person who harbors it and destroys his or her relationships with others. This is an obvious threat to family wholeness and well-being, and it grows directly out of a lack of understanding of Christian virtues such as grace and forgiveness.

Good parenting requires understanding, patience, direction, wisdom, and perseverance.

Social Issues
Confronting the Family

Many of the personal problems affecting our own families are rooted in something bigger—namely, society's shifting worldview. Ideas matter, and, for better or worse, people nowadays tend to get most of their ideas about the meaning of life and the purpose of institutions like marriage and the family from popular social norms.

There was a time when Christian principles and biblical values were regarded as the unchallenged foundation of Western culture. This is sadly no longer the case. As our society has drifted away from its earlier moral and spiritual moorings, many of the things we once considered self-evident truths have come into question. This in turn has spelled trouble for the family and the stability of the home. Here are some of the most significant ways in which this shift in social attitudes has made itself felt in family life.

Marriage deemed a personal or sentimental idea.

In chapters 1 and 2 we defined marriage as a "one-flesh" union between a woman and a man that uniquely reflects the image of God. We've also seen that it is meant to be a permanent, lifelong commitment deserving honor in good times and bad, and it is a public institution that involves a commitment to the larger community, forming the basic building block of human society. In recent times, these hallmarks of marriage have been replaced with individualistic ideas. For many people today, marriage is primarily a matter of personal happiness and fulfillment.

Any marriage that doesn't provide self-satisfaction isn't worth keeping, so we throw it away and look for greener grass.

Individualism. We've already discussed the "me first" attitude as a problem in family life. All that remains to be said here is that this mentality is part of a larger cultural trend. Self-denial and service to others are not popular values today. Polonius's dictum "To thine own self be true" has replaced Donne's "No man is an island" as the mantra of the age. This is truly a social cancer.

Antinatalism. There is at present a troubling trend away from bearing and raising children. A number of years ago, the National Marriage Project stated that "demographically, socially, and culturally, the nation is shifting from a society of child-rearing families to a society of child-free adults."[51] This is significant. As demographer Phillip Longman warns, "No industrialized nation still produces enough children to sustain its population over time, or to prevent rapid population aging."[52] This unfortunate trend flows from an attitude that says "children are a problem to be avoided," hence driving the genocide of abortion. Such an attitude contradicts the biblical teaching that children are a precious gift from God (Psalm 127:3) and that every baby is a new, unique bearer of God's very image in the world. No wonder Satan is targeting new human life so destructively.

Divorce. Our nation's forty-year experiment with no-fault divorce has made one thing clear: Divorce is far more harmful to men, women, and children than even the most conservative critics could have imagined when it began. We now live in a world where it's easier to get out of a thirty-year marriage than a two-week-old cell phone contract. The negative impact on individual lives has been devastating. Divorce tears apart not just the man and woman who had become "one flesh," but also an entire family, and every member in that family. This is why God hates divorce.

Superfluous fathers. Fatherlessness is a serious social problem. More than 25 percent of children in America now live in a home where the father has either left or was never present.[53] This is extremely bad news for kids. Social science data consistently shows that a father's involvement in the lives of his children is irreplaceable.

Cohabitation. "Living together" outside of marriage is now the Western world's fastest growing family formation trend, having increased seventeenfold in the United States since 1960.[54] Researchers tell us that this living arrangement is functionally distinct from and far less healthy and stable than marriage. The reason, according to many sociologists, is that cohabitation promotes more individualistic attitudes and confused expectations among couples with regard to the future of their relationship.

Same-sex marriage and families. As we have pointed out, the pairing of male and female is fundamental to God's plan, since *both* are His image in the world in similar (human) but also different (gender-distinct) ways. Same-sex marriage challenges this divine reality. All societies need both genders to make a marriage a human whole. Apart from the theological and moral issues involved, a compassionate society never intentionally creates fatherless or motherless homes. But this is exactly what we have in same-sex families, and solely to fulfill the desires and wishes of the adults who form them.

Polygamy and multi-partner marriage.

A recent multi-disciplinary study conducted by a small group of psychologists, economists, and anthropologists from the University of British Columbia, UCLA, and UC Davis asserts that the encouragement and enforcement of monogamy has important implications for the health of a culture in terms of safety, productivity, healthy child development, and father involvement.[55] All this is under threat in our society, where so-called polyamory (defined by *Webster*'s as "having more than one open romantic relationship at a time") is an increasing trend, and where the possibility of legalized polygamy is once again raising its head on the political, legal, and cultural horizon.

Premarital and extramarital sex.

C. S. Lewis wrote, "The monstrosity of sexual intercourse outside marriage is that those who indulge in it are trying to isolate one kind of union (the sexual) from all the other kinds of union which were intended to go along with it and make up the total union."[56] Unfortunately, as the heirs of the 1960s "sexual revolution," we now live in a society where sex outside of marriage seems to have become the norm (or so the media would have us believe).

Artificial (or assisted) reproductive technology.

In vitro fertilization, surrogacy, and other forms of artificial reproduction technology can help facilitate conception for married couples facing infertility. Some of these techniques can also be considered ethically acceptable from a Christian point of view, provided the couple does not go outside the relationship to obtain reproductive material and resources.[57]

But such technology can also foster an impersonal, disembodied approach to procreation for singles and same-sex couples. This contradicts the whole idea of marriage and family.

Conclusion

These threats to the family are not imaginary. They're very real, and we are facing them now. Contemporary cultural and societal trends have combined to aggravate the pressures that naturally go along with family life. That's why it's no exaggeration to say that the family is "under attack" in our time as never before.

So our work is cut out for us. If we want to help families thrive, we can't sit back and leave the outcome to chance. We have to find practical ways to counterbalance the negative forces and trends with positive, healthy, redeeming values. We need a plan. We need a strategy. *And we have one.*

When I was divorced, I was faced with rearing two daughters, nine and three years old. My younger daughter was a classic headstrong child on the way to what I was sure was a very troubled teenhood. She had a lot of anger and confusion. I knew she was unhappy, and I could feel her reaching out. I needed to learn how to reach back.

Through various programs on Focus's radio show—one specifically by Cynthia Tobias—I learned to change my parenting style. I learned that it was through love and support, talking instead of yelling, and most of all, through listening to my daughter, that our relationship could turn the corner and become full of positive interaction. I learned the value of a hug. I learned how to help my daughter work through what she was feeling, and to express that in more productive ways.

I am very happy to say that I recently dropped off my daughter at Florida State University after she graduated from high school summa cum laude. She is a delight. I can't say enough about the joy I have had in being the mother to both of my daughters.

Thank you, Focus on the Family, for seeing me through those crucial single-parenting years. Because of you, I learned how to parent differently and now enjoy relationships with my daughters that other people envy. You saved my life and the life of my family!

—*Actual letter (name withheld)*

Chapter 6
Helping Families Thrive

Focus on the Family's Five Strategic Priorities

I want to tell you about how a recent Focus broadcast spoke directly into my severely troubled marriage. I had reached a point where my bags were packed and I was just "waiting for the right time" to leave my marriage of 32 years. My husband travels extensively. One morning he called from the road to ask me to listen to the Focus on the Family program that he had just heard. He said that as he listened to the discussion with the studio guests, he realized the message—about the danger of other life pursuits becoming a "mistress" that plunders the relationship with one's spouse—was describing him. The Lord touched his heart and showed him that he has been prioritizing many other things in life at the expense of our marriage. I could feel a change in my husband as he was talking, which is a huge answer to years of prayer! I am so excited about the possibilities for our relationship and want you to know that lives are being changed through your ministry.

—A Focus listener

Here at Focus on the Family we're all about helping families thrive in Christ. By God's grace, we're working to enable moms, dads, and kids to become everything they can be within the parameters of the Creator's beautiful design. As we've seen, there are both positive and negative aspects to this task.

On the one hand, we're doing everything we can to help couples establish healthy marriages that reflect God's plan. We're also coming alongside parents in active, practical ways as they seek to raise their children according to biblical principles. We give families the tools they need to build strong, loving households on a firm, godly foundation.

On the other hand, we're consciously engaged in helping families protect themselves from harmful influences in modern culture. We want them to understand the obstacles they're facing so they can arm themselves against social forces that are hostile to family life. Ultimately, our purpose in this area is to equip moms, dads, and kids to make a greater difference in the lives of those around them.

Just how do we accomplish all this? That's a question we've thought much about over the years. Out of our thinking and pondering—and the hard-won experience that has accompanied it—we've come up with a plan. We like to talk about that plan in terms of *Five Strategic Priorities*: *Evangelism*, *Marriage*, *Parenting*, *Advocacy for Children*, and *Engaging the Culture*. In the remaining pages of this booklet we want to do two things:

1 Briefly explain the vision and the rationale for each component of the plan.

2 Show you how real people's lives and families have been helped through our dedication to the Five Strategic Priorities.

Evangelism

Our efforts to "focus on the family" are actually subservient to a larger, more fundamental, all-inclusive goal. We're primarily engaged in an evangelistic endeavor and have been since our founding. We want people to know the Lord, and we believe that encouraging and helping build strong families is a highly strategic way to do this, as most people who come to Christ have been influenced in that direction in some way by their family experiences. We have a vision to glorify God in all we do, introduce people to Jesus Christ, and provide them the tools they need in order to share the good news with others.

Are we succeeding in this area? We believe so. An enthusiastic friend of the ministry stopped by to tell us what our outreach had meant to her and her son during a very dark period in their lives. Here's what she had to say:

My husband committed suicide in our home, and my 10-year-old son discovered his body. The grief and agony were overwhelming, especially because we had no family or close friends to turn to for comfort. I had heard of Focus on the Family and, out of desperation, decided to reach out to your ministry, even though I knew very little about you. I poured out my heart in a letter and put it in the mail. A short time later, I received an uplifting and encouraging box of materials from your ministry and a personal phone call from one of the counselors on your staff. My son was surprised to receive his own box as well. Inside were a children's Bible, a set of *Adventures in Odyssey* dramas, and several other resources geared to kids.

The story doesn't end there. Alone in his room, my son began reading his Bible, watching the videos, and listening to the *Odyssey* stories. On his own, he prayed to receive the Lord Jesus Christ as his Savior. Then he said, "Mommy, you need Jesus too." So I got on my knees and prayed with him to receive Christ into my life. For two years I saved a little money here and there so we could take a trip to Focus on the Family. We just wanted to be able to tell you "thank you" in person for caring.

We are blessed and humbled to hear many stories like this every week.

Marriage

A fervent desire to bolster the God-ordained institution of marriage is central to everything we do at Focus on the Family. We have a vision to come alongside spouses and those who are not yet married, helping them develop a sound understanding of the Lord's design for marriage. We also want to equip couples with a resiliency that will enable them to weather the storms of marriage. We teach them the skills and habits they need to establish a strong, intimate relationship—one that demonstrates the meaning of marriage and family to a hurting world, as well as to their children.

Are we making a measurable difference in the marriages of men and women who turn to us for assistance? The following writer is just one of many who've given a resounding yes.

I have been a devout Christian for many years, but after over thirty years of marriage, I was beginning to despair of ever truly being happily married the way I had hoped to be when I first met my husband. We looked okay from the outside, I guess. But for nearly a decade, I had stopped trying to talk to my husband.

I had reached a point where I began to cry out to God, unable to keep going. I could really see how even devout Christians might contemplate divorce. Then one day, while driving in my car with the Christian radio station on, I happened to hear your broadcast. Dr. Emerson Eggerichs was talking about men and why they are the way they are, and why they react the way they do. I was awestruck by the message. It filled my soul with a feeling of incredible hope.

I began to put this scriptural advice into practice. As a result, the marriage of my dreams started to unfold. My husband saw the change in me, and I shared with him a bit of what I was learning. He loved the message he was hearing. As we put that message into practice and saw how well it worked, we began to share it with friends. We have now done a number of Love and Respect house groups, as well as a conference in a larger setting.

Instead of an angry, shut-down man, my husband is now funny, adoring, and kind. I've changed for the better, too. Thanks to all of you who make this kind of material available to those who need it!

Parenting

When men and women come together within the bond of marriage, children are usually the result. This, too, is part of God's design. And this, as we've said, is where family begins. From a certain perspective, birthing and raising children is what family is all about. The vision for Focus on the Family's parenting ministry is to come alongside moms and dads and equip them to train up the next generation to live in the power of a transformational Christian faith.

Here again, we've heard from thousands of parents who assure us that our broadcasts, articles, books, and other practical child-rearing advice have provided them with the strength and wisdom they need to raise healthy, God-fearing children. The woman who sent the following note is a good example.

When my husband and I were new parents of a baby girl, we ventured off to South Dakota, far from our familiar Wyoming upbringing. I spent two months in this new place on my own while my husband attended training out of town. I was hungry for companionship but knew no one. I found your radio show on a local station and began to tune in faithfully. You were my lifeline. Through Focus, I have gained parenting skills that have blessed our family in many ways. My own mother has said to me, "I have learned more about how to parent children by watching you than I ever knew in my whole life."

This is a credit to you, Focus on the Family. That is the blessing you offered to a young mom who desperately wanted to know how to raise her kids "right." As the years have passed, I have often found myself offering your advice to other young moms who are in the same boat. Your impact in my life has gone well beyond my own household. I have a deep, unwavering admiration and love for what you have done for me and for millions of others around the world.

Advocacy
for Children

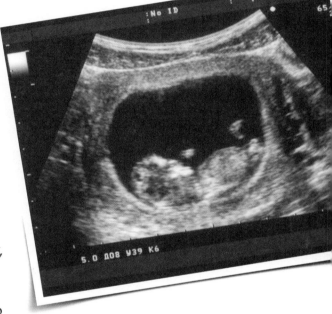

Because we understand the high value that Scripture places on children, we're involved in spreading the message that kids are a blessing, not only to their own families but also to the local community, the nation, and the world at large. We speak up for children who can't speak for themselves, and we equip our friends and supporters to do the same. We at Focus are doing what we can to save the lives of preborn children, to preserve the value of human life in all its stages, and to encourage loving families to provide lasting homes for orphaned children.

One of the most remarkable notes we've received in this regard came from an embryologist. Here's what he said about the impact our message has had on his ideas concerning the sanctity of human life.

As an embryologist, I participate in inseminating eggs retrieved from women (in vitro fertilization or IVF), growing embryos, transferring embryos to women, and freezing, storing, and thawing embryos. Among other things, I'm responsible for overseeing the frozen embryo storage program. I track hundreds of patients who collectively have thousands of embryos stored at our clinic.

When I first started my work, I hadn't given a great deal of thought to the question of when life actually begins. As time passed and I became more involved with the embryo storage program, I found myself wondering more and more about the embryos I was processing. What exactly were they? Were they just cellular matter like the cells in our cheeks or like red blood cells? Were they potential life? Were they life, period?

Over the years I have literally thrown away hundreds of embryos. Most are discarded because couples now have a "complete family" and do not intend to have any more children. They do not have the courage to donate the embryos to other couples, because the thought of someone else raising "their child" is too disturbing. And they think donating to research is "barbaric." As a result, discarding is the most logical and practical solution for them.

Throwing away embryos that were perfectly good became a burden for me. As the burden grew, I searched harder for an answer to the question of when life begins. I also wanted to find a better way of dealing with the large number of stored embryos at our clinic. My searching led me to read a book published by Focus on the Family—*Unplanned*, by Abby Johnson. I found this book to be encouraging and incredibly applicable to my situation. I also began praying for peace and direction.

The upshot? I have told my supervisor that I will no longer participate in discarding embryos. She supports that. She's also in favor of re-examining embryo disposition on a clinic-wide level and finding out how other workers feel about the procedure. I will continue to explore ways to reduce the chance that couples will have to even consider discarding embryos. I feel I am being pulled in a direction involving embryo donation or IVF counseling, but I cannot clearly see the path. What I can see is that God is in charge of all of this. I trust Him to guide me down the path, wherever it may lead.

God is moving and guiding, even in these very "advanced" scientific areas.

Engaging *the Culture*

Is there anything we can do to counter the negative influences of a culture that has drifted from its biblical roots? Are there loving, caring, winsome, and positive steps we can take, both on a national and a personal level, to confront those forces

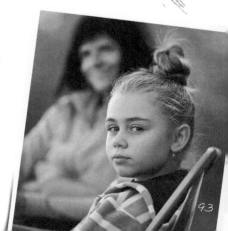

that are undermining the family in modern society? We're convinced that there are. Our overarching vision in the area of cultural engagement entails equipping families to influence their communities through biblical citizenship. As we see it, this effort involves elements drawn from all our other strategic priorities: strengthening and defending marriage, training and supporting parents, advocating for children, and—above all—sharing the gospel with those who don't know the Lord.

How are we doing in the cultural arena? The woman who wrote the following letter seemed to have benefited from our work.

> For many years I have stood on my own soapbox about why I don't vote, yet I am disgusted at what our government has become. Feeling that I have no power as an individual to make a difference with just a lonely check mark, I have battled within myself whether to register and vote.
>
> But after listening to your broadcast this morning, I was filled with conviction of my selfish perspective; I'd failed to see the whole picture. Now I know how important my check mark is, not just for one president but for a slew of issues.
>
> This is not a time to sulk and cry but to stand firm in our faith that affects so much around us. I know my faith in God needs to remain steadfast, and His sovereignty will prevail in the end. I will continue to pray for the president, our country, and those who fail to accept God for who He truly is. May the Holy Spirit continue to fill you every day to accurately spread His truths.

What Can You Do to Help?

This, then, is a snapshot of what we're all about here at Focus on the Family. Obviously, there's a lot more that could be said. We haven't had time or space in this booklet to go into detail. But we have hit the high points. We've told and showed you why we believe that family is so important. It is both a God issue and a human issue, and it is the latter because of the former. We've also explained what we're doing to help families thrive. Now there's just one thing left to say: We need your help.

If you've caught a vision for spreading the good news of Jesus Christ through family outreach—if you believe, as we do, that healthy, intact families are part of God's plan for the well-being of all mankind—then we want you to join us in the work. There are a number of ways you can do this. Here are just a few suggestions.

Make sure your own family is strong and thriving.

You can keep moving in this direction by listening to Focus on the Family broadcasts, visiting our website, and taking advantage of the many books, magazines, and other resources we offer.

Understand why marriage and family matter, and what can be done to promote, protect, and preserve these God-given institutions. In this booklet you've had a quick but solid introduction to the topic. Now go out and make yourself an expert.

Help your church and the families in your community by sharing your knowledge and organizing local efforts to strengthen homes and promote the message of biblically based family values.

Host a marriage group or a parenting study in your home. Invite both your Christian friends and your non-Christian neighbors. We have a wealth of resources that can help. Please call us at 1-800-A-FAMILY.

Mentor a young engaged or married couple, especially if their marriage is struggling. Young couples today are perhaps the first generation to have so few positive examples of good marriages in their own families and among their friends' parents. They are desperately looking for couples who can give them hope, help, and encouragement in their marriages. And they are not looking for "perfect" couples as mentors. They want mentors who have overcome real struggles together.

Be culturally savvy. Inform yourself about the corrosive forces harming families in present-day society, and take steps to counteract them.

Support organizations like Focus on the Family with your prayers and your financial contributions. God has called us to accomplish this task together, and we can't possibly do what He's asked us to do without your backing and assistance.

Family matters. It matters because, as Chesterton said, the family is the factory that manufactures humanity. It matters because the future passes by way of the family. It matters because the health and well-being of the entire world rises and falls with the health and well-being of the home.

Let's get together and do something about it!

We can't do it alone, and we would be most honored to have your partnership.

God's Wisdom for Your Family

The Word of God provides divine and timeless wisdom for families everywhere. It guides husbands and wives in shaping their life together, parents in raising and caring for their sons and daughters, and children in honoring and obeying their parents. Paying attention to God's instruction on the family is a wise way to build strong marriages, raise happy children, and maintain thriving homes. Every community needs this.

For Marriage

So God created man in his own image, in the image of God he created him; male and female he created them.

And God blessed them. And God said to them, "Be fruitful and multiply and fill the earth and subdue it. . . ."

(Genesis 1:27-28; see also 9:1, 7; 17:20; 28:3; 35:11; 48:4)

God's creation of man and woman was also the creation of marriage. When Adam was alone at first, God said it wasn't good, though the apostle Paul later taught that celibacy too can be a gift from God (1 Corinthians 7:6-10). Marriage is the norm. And marriages are to be fruitful in love between the husband and wife, leading to a new generation of God's unique image-bearers: children.

For Husbands

Husbands, love your wives, as Christ loved the church and gave himself up for her, that he might sanctify her. . . . In the same way husbands should love their wives as their own bodies. He who loves his wife loves himself. For no one ever hated his own flesh, but nourishes and cherishes it, just as Christ does the church, because we are members of his body.

(Ephesians 5:25-30)

Every husband is commanded to love his wife, putting her needs before his own, even to the point of dying for her, just as Christ loved, served, and died for the church. This is a tough calling for husbands, but it is God's command.

For Wives

Wives, submit to your own husbands, as to the Lord. For the husband is the head of the wife even as Christ is the head of the church, his body, and is himself its Savior. Now as the church submits to Christ, so also wives should submit in everything to their husbands.

(Ephesians 5:22-24)

Likewise, wives, be subject to your own husbands, so that even if some do not obey the word, they may be won without a word by the conduct of their wives, when they see your respectful and pure conduct. . . . For this is how the holy women who hoped in God used to adorn themselves, by submitting to their own husbands, as Sarah obeyed Abraham, calling him lord. And you are her children, if you do good and do not fear anything that is frightening.

(1 Peter 3:1-2, 5-6)

Wives are to respect the authority of their husbands, similar to the manner in which the church should respect Christ's authority. Jesus's rule over the church is not tyrannical, but loving and redemptive. Faithful wives are a living example of the way the church is commanded to relate to Christ.

For Parents

"And these words that I command you today shall be on your heart. You shall teach them diligently to your children, and shall talk of them when you sit in your house, and when you walk by the way, and when you lie down, and when you rise."

(Deuteronomy 6:6-7)

Fathers and mothers are told to fervently instruct their children—within the home and in the community—about the laws established in God's Word. This means raising children who obey their parents not just by their outer behavior but also from their hearts.

"You shall not bow down [to other gods] or serve them, for I the LORD your God am a jealous God, visiting the iniquity of the fathers on the children to the third and the fourth generation of those who hate me, but showing steadfast love to thousands of those who love me and keep my commandments."

(Exodus 20:5-6; Deuteronomy 5:9)

A father is to guard his own heart, mind, and behavior so he doesn't end up involving his children and grandchildren in his own sin. In God's eyes, every family is part of a generational history. This places each father under a significant obligation.

Did [the LORD] not make them [husband and wife] one, with a portion of the Spirit in their union? And what was the one God seeking? Godly offspring.

(Malachi 2:15)

God has brought husband and wife together as one flesh to give Him godly children, which He is seeking. That is a big responsibility for mothers and fathers.

Fathers, do not provoke your children to anger, but bring them up in the discipline and instruction of the Lord.

(Ephesians 6:4)

Fathers are to guide their children with a gentle faithfulness. They should avoid upsetting their children needlessly, but use only the proper discipline needed for spiritual training.

He must manage his own household well, with all dignity
keeping his children submissive, for if someone does not know how
to manage his own household, how will he care for God's church?

(1 Timothy 3:4-5)

Wise and loving leadership is so important to God that He requires those who want to be leaders in the church to first demonstrate proper leadership within their own families. And no family is perfect, so perfection is not the goal, but rather diligence and faithfulness.

For Children, Young and Old

Therefore a man shall leave his father and his mother and
hold fast to his wife, and they shall become one flesh.

(Genesis 2:24; see also Ephesians 5:31)

Men and women who marry should put each other's welfare before all other relationships, even that of their parents. They, man and woman, should also consummate their union through the marital embrace. They literally and mysteriously become one flesh.

"'Honor your father and your mother, as the LORD your God
commanded you, that your days may be long, and that it may go
well with you in the land that the LORD your God is giving you.'"

(Deuteronomy 5:16; see also Exodus 20:12; Ephesians 6:1-3)

Children are commanded by God to honor their parents. Doing so leads to long life, because this is how God meant for every human being to grow and mature.

Notes

1. G. K. Chesterton, *The Superstition of Divorce* (Whitefish, MT: Kessinger, 2003), 66.

2. Edward Westermarck, *The History of Human Marriage* (New York: Allerton Book Company, 1922), 1:26, 46, 27.

3. Margaret Mead, *Male and Female: A Study of the Sexes in a Changing World* (New York: HarperCollins, 2001), 174.

4. Benjamin Scafidi, *The Taxpayer Costs of Divorce and Unwed Childbearing: First-Ever Estimates for the Nation and All Fifty States* (New York: Institute for American Values/ Georgia Family Council, 2008), 17.

5. Colin E. Gunton, *The Promise of Trinitarian Theology*, 2nd ed. (London: T&T Clark, 1997), 3, 7.

6. Michael Downey, *Altogether Gift: A Trinitarian Spirituality* (Maryknoll, NY: Orbis Books, 2000), 63.

7. Adapted from Dr. Kevin Leman, *Home Court Advantage* (Carol Stream, IL: Tyndale/Focus on the Family, 2005), 129-30.

8. From Steve Wade, in Glenn T. Stanton, *My Crazy Imperfect Christian Family* (Colorado Springs: NavPress, 2004), 34–36.

9. T. Berry Brazelton and Stanley I. Greenspan, *The Irreducible Needs of Children: What Every Child Must Have to Grow, Learn, and Flourish* (Cambridge, MA: Da Capo Press, 2000); Council of Economic Advisers, *Teens and Their Parents in the 21st Century: An Examination of Trends in Teen Behavior and the Role of Parental Involvement* (Washington, DC: Council of Economic Advisers, 2000); John DeFrain, "Strong Families Around the World," *Family Matters* 53 (Winter 1999): 6–13; Marla E. Eisenberg et al., "Correlations Between Family Meals and Psychosocial Well-Being Among Adolescents," *Archives of Pediatric and Adolescent Medicine* 158 (August 2004): 792–96; Frank D. Fincham et al., "Spiritual Behaviors and Relationship Satisfaction: A Critical Analysis of the Role of Prayer," *Journal of Social and Clinical Psychology* 27, no. 4 (2008): 362–88; Lawrence E. Gary et al., *Stable Black Families: Final Report* (Washington, DC: Mental Health Research and Development Center/Institute for Urban Affairs and Research/Howard University, 1983); Robert B. Hill, *The Strengths of Black Families*, 2nd ed. (Lanham, MD: University Press of America, 2003); Vincent Jeffries, "Religiosity, Benevolent Love, and Long-Lasting Marriages," *Humboldt Journal of Social Relations* 30, no. 1 (2006): 77–106; Jerry M. Lewis, *How's Your Family: A Guide to Identifying Your Family's Strengths and Weaknesses* (New York: Brunner/Mazel, 1979); Kristin Anderson Moore et al., "Family Strengths: Often Overlooked, but Real," *Child Trends Research Briefs* (Washington, DC: Child Trends, 2002); CASA, *The Importance of Family Dinners IV* (New York: National Center on Addiction and Substance Abuse at Columbia University, 2007); David H. Olson et al., *Families: What Makes Them Work*, 2nd ed. (Newbury Park, CA: Sage Publications, 1989); Suzanna Smith, "Building a Strong and Resilient Family," University of Florida IFAS Extension, no. FCS2057 (2005); Nick Stinnett and John DeFrain, *Secrets of Strong Families* (Boston: Little, Brown, 1985); Brenda J. Thames, "Building Family Strengths: Overview," Clemson University Cooperative Extension Service, no. FL 520, January 1998.

10 Christian Smith, *Souls in Transition: The Religious and Spiritual Lives of Emerging Adults* (New York: Oxford University Press, 2009), 220–24.

11 Adapted from Gordon McLean, *Too Young to Die* (Wheaton, IL: Tyndale/Focus on the Family, 1998), 24–27.

12 G. K. Chesterton, "The Policeman as a Mother," *The New Witness*, November 14, 1919.

13 Linda J. Waite and Maggie Gallagher, *The Case for Marriage: Why Married People Are Happier, Healthier, and Better Off Financially* (New York: Doubleday, 2000), 64.

14 M. Koskenvuo et al., "Differences in Mortality from Ischemic Heart Disease by Marital Status and Social Class," *Journal of Chronic Diseases* 33, no. 2 (1980): 95–106; Lois M. Verbrugge, "Marital Status and Health," *Journal of Marriage and Family* 41, no. 2 (May 1979): 267–85; James J. Lynch, *The Broken Heart: The Medical Consequences of Loneliness* (New York, Basic Books, 1977); in Robert H. Coombs, "Marital Status and Personal Well-Being: A Literature Review," *Family Relations* 40, no. 1 (January 1991): 97–102.

15 Steven Stack and J. Ross Eshleman, "Marital Status and Happiness: A Seventeen-Nation Study," *Journal of Marriage and Family* 60, no. 2 (May 1998): 527, 534.

16 Susan L. Brown, "The Effect of Union Type on Psychological Well-Being: Depression Among Cohabitors Versus Marrieds," *Journal of Health and Social Behavior* 41, no. 3 (September 2000): 241.

17 Walter R. Gove, "The Relationship Between Sex Roles, Mental Illness, and Marital Status," *Social Forces* 51 (1972): 34–44; Robert T. Seagraves, "Marriage and Mental Health," *Journal of Sex and Marital Therapy* 6 (1980): 187–98; in David R. Williams, David T. Takeuchi, and Russell K. Adair, "Marital Status and Psychiatric Disorders Among Blacks and Whites," *Journal of Health and Social Behavior* 33, no. 2 (June 1992): 141.

18 David G. Blanchflower and Andrew J. Oswald, "Well-Being over Time in Britain and the USA," *Journal of Public Economics* 88, nos. 7–8 (July 2004): 1359–86, cited in Chris M. Wilson and Andrew J. Oswald, "How Does Marriage Affect Physical and Psychological Health? A Survey of Longitudinal Evidence," Institute for the Study of Labor, discussion paper no. 1619 (May 2005): 1.

19 Janet Wilmoth and Gregor Koso, "Does Marital History Matter? Marital Status and Wealth Outcomes Among Preretirement Adults," *Journal of Marriage and Family* 64, no. 1 (February 2002): 261.

20 George A. Akerlof, "Men Without Children," *The Economic Journal* 108, no. 447 (March 1998): 304.

21 Robert T. Michael et al., *Sex in America: A Definitive Survey* (Boston: Little, Brown, 1994), 131; see also Edward O. Laumann et al., *The Social Organization of Sexuality: Sexual Practices in the United States* (Chicago: University of Chicago Press, 1994), 364, table 10.5; Andrew M. Greeley, *Faithful Attraction: Discovering Intimacy, Love, and Fidelity in American Marriage* (New York: Tor/Tom Doherty Associates, 1991), chapter 6.

22 Greeley, *Faithful Attraction*, 97–98, 143–45.

23 Kristin Anderson Moore et al., "Marriage from a Child's Perspective: How Does Family Structure Affect Children, and What Can We Do About It?" *Child Trends Research Brief* (June 2002): 1–2.

24 Trude Bennett, "Marital Status and Infant Health Outcomes," *Social Science and Medicine* 35, no. 9 (November 1992): 1179–87.

25 In Sweden: A. Arntzen et al., "Marital Status as a Risk Factor for Fetal and Infant Mortality," *Scandinavian Journal of Social Medicine* 24, no. 1 (1996): 36–42; in England: Jeremy Schuman, "Childhood, Infant, and Perinatal Mortality, 1996: Social and Biological Factors in Deaths of Children Aged Under Three," *Population Trends* 92 (Summer 1998): 8–9; in Finland: Erja Forssas et al., "Maternal Predictors of Perinatal Mortality: The Role of Birth Weight," *International Journal of Epidemiology* 28, no. 3 (June 1999): 475–78.

26 Deborah A. Dawson, "Family Structure and Children's Health and Well-Being: Data from the 1988 National Health Interview Survey on Child Health," *Journal of Marriage and Family* 53, no. 3 (August 1991): 579.

27 Judith S. Wallerstein, Julia M. Lewis, and Sandra Blakeslee, *The Unexpected Legacy of Divorce: A Twenty-Five-Year Landmark Study* (New York: Hyperion, 2000), xxix–xxxi, xxxiii–xxxv.

28 Sara McLanahan and Gary Sandefur, *Growing Up with a Single Parent: What Hurts, What Helps* (Cambridge, MA: Harvard University Press, 1994), chapter 2; Wendy Sigle-Rushton and Sara McLanahan, "Father Absence and Child Well-Being: A Critical Review," Center for Research on Child Wellbeing, Princeton University, working paper no. 02-20 (November 2002), http://www.policyarchive.org/handle/10207/bitstreams/21760.pdf.

29 Ronald P. Rohner and Robert A. Veneziano, "The Importance of Father Love: History and Contemporary Evidence," *Review of General Psychology* 5, no. 4 (December 2001): 382.

30 Jonathan Rauch, "The Widening Marriage Gap: America's New Class Divide," *National Journal*, May 19, 2001, http://reason.com/archives/2001/05/19/the-widening-marriage-gap-amer.

31 W. Bradford Wilcox et al., *Why Marriage Matters: Twenty-Six Conclusions from the Social Sciences*, rev. ed. (New York: Institute of American Values, 2005), 19.

32 James S. Coleman et al., *Equality of Educational Opportunity* (Washington DC: US Government Printing Office, 1966), chapter 3.

33 Elizabeth Thomson, Thomas L. Hanson, and Sara S. McLanahan, "Family Structure and Child Well-Being: Economic Resources vs. Parental Behaviors," *Social Forces* 73, no. 1 (September 1994): 227, 237, in Daniel P. Moynihan, Timothy M. Smeeding, and Lee Rainwater eds., *The Future of the Family* (New York: Russell Sage Foundation, 2004), 121.

34 McLanahan and Sandefur, *Growing Up with a Single Parent*, 44–45; Moynihan, Smeeding, and Rainwater, *The Future of the Family*, 121–22.

35 McLanahan and Sandefur, *Growing Up with a Single Parent*, 47.

36 Susan L. Brown, "Family Structure and Child Well-Being: The Significance of Parental Cohabitation," *Journal of Marriage and Family* 66, no. 2 (May 2004): 351–67.

37 Paula Fomby and Andrew J. Cherlin, "Family Instability and Child Well-Being," *American Sociological Review* 72, no. 2 (April 2007): 181–204; Hyun Sik Kim, "Consequences of Parental Divorce for Child Development," *American Sociological Review* 76, no. 3 (June 2011): 487–511.

38 Wendy D. Manning, Pamela J. Smock, and Debarun Majumdar, "The Relative Stability of Cohabiting and Marital Unions for Children," *Population Research and Policy Review* 23, no. 2 (April 2004): 151.

39 Nanette K. Gartrell, Henny M. W. Bos, and Naomi G. Goldberg, "Adolescents of the

US National Longitudinal Lesbian Family Study: Sexual Orientation, Sexual Behavior, and Sexual Risk Exposure," *Archive of Sexual Behavior* 40, no. 6 (December 2011): 1199–209.

40 Timothy J. Biblarz and Judith Stacey, "How Does the Gender of Parents Matter?" *Journal of Marriage and Family* 72, no. 1 (February 2010): 3–22; Gunnar Andersson et al., "The Demographics of Same-Sex Marriages in Norway and Sweden," *Demography* 43, no. 1 (February 2006): 79–98.

41 Moynihan, Smeeding, and Rainwater, *The Future of the Family*, 126.

42 Wilcox, *Why Marriage Matters*, 29.

43 Robert J. Sampson, "Urban Black Violence: The Effect of Male Joblessness and Family Disruption," *American Journal of Sociology* 93, no. 2 (September 1987): 348–82, in Michael R. Gottfredson and Travis Hirschi, *A General Theory of Crime* (Stanford, CA: Stanford University Press, 1990), 103.

44 Rohner and Veneziano, "The Importance of Father Love," 382–405; Kyle D. Pruett, *Fatherneed: Why Father Care Is as Essential as Mother Care for Your Child* (New York: Free Press, 2000); Henry B. Biller, *Father and Families: Paternal Factors in Child Development* (Westport, CT: Auburn House, 1993); Ross Parke, *Fatherhood* (Cambridge, MA: Harvard University Press, 1996).

45 Michael N. Stiffman et al., "Household Composition and Risk of Fatal Child Maltreatment," *Pediatrics* 109, no. 4 (April 2002): 615–21.

46 US Department of Justice, "Criminal Victimization in the United States, 2007 Statistical Tables," *National Crime Victimization Survey*, Bureau of Justice Statistics NCJ 227669, February 2010, tables 11–12.

47 Robert L. Flewelling and Karl E. Bauman, "Family Structure as a Predictor of Initial Substance Use and Sexual Intercourse in Early Adolescence," *Journal of Marriage and Family* 52, no. 1 (February 1990): 171–81; Robert A. Johnson, John P. Hoffman, and Dean R. Gerstein, *The Relationship Between Family Structure and Adolescent Substance Use* (Rockville, MD: Substance Abuse and Mental Health Services Administrations, Office of Applied Studies/US Department of Health and Human Services, 1996), 2.

48 James Q. Wilson, *The Marriage Problem: How Our Culture Has Weakened Families* (New York: HarperCollins, 2002), 7.

49 Adapted from Betsy Holt and Mike Yorkey, *Always* (Wheaton, IL: Tyndale/Focus on the Family, 1999), 77–100.

50 Andreas J. Köstenberger, *God, Marriage, and Family: Rebuilding the Biblical Foundation*, 2nd ed. (Wheaton, IL: Crossway, 2010), 15.

51 Barbara Dafoe Whitehead and David Popenoe, *Life Without Children: The Social Retreat from Children and How It Is Changing America* (Piscataway, NJ: National Marriage Project/Rutgers, 2008), 30.

52 Phillip Longman, *The Empty Cradle: How Falling Birthrates Threaten World Prosperity and What to Do About It* (New York: Basic Books, 2004), 8.

53 US Census Bureau, "America's Families and Living Arrangements: 2012," *Current Population Survey: 2012 Annual Social and Economic Supplement* (Washington, DC: US Government Printing Office, 2012), table C9, http://www.census.gov/hhes/families/data/cps2012.html.

54 US Census Bureau, "Families and Living Arrangements: Historical Time Series— Living Arrangements of Adults," *Current Population Survey: March and Annual Social and Economic Supplements, 2012 and Earlier*

(Washington, DC: US Government Printing Office, 2012), table UC-1, http://www. census.gov/hhes/families/data/adults.html.

55 Joseph Henrich, Robert Boyd, and Peter J. Richerson, "The Puzzle of Monogamous Marriage," *Philosophical Transactions: Biological Sciences* 367, no. 1589 (March 2012): 657–69.

56 C. S. Lewis, *Mere Christianity* (New York: Macmillan, 1960), 96.

57 A possible exception to this would be embryo adoption, where a couple is providing a home—albeit in the womb and after birth—for an orphaned human embryo. Of course, this is not God's ideal, as orphans never are, but this is a result of our brave new and troubling world of reproductive technology.

You can help build
STRONGER FAMILIES
through your
LOYAL SUPPORT

We want to invite you to join a special group of our most loyal supporters, called *Friends of the Family.*

You'll receive special members–only resources and the joy of knowing you're investing in stronger families — including yours! Your monthly gift will provide counsel, media and printed resources to:

- Build strong, lasting marriages
- Instill faith in children
- Promote a pro-family perspective in our culture and much more!

Best of all, your *Friends of the Family* membership will make sure that families that can't afford the assistance they need won't be left out. If you're already a *Friend of the Family,* thank you for making this life-changing ministry possible.

To join Friends of the Family now, visit FocusOnTheFamily.com/WhyFamilyMatters or call 800-A-FAMILY

Colorado Springs, CO 80920 • 800-A-FAMILY (232-6459)
FocusOnTheFamily.com/WhyFamilyMatters

FOCUS ON THE FAMILY

Helping Families Thrive

THE PROFOUND IMPACT OF BIBLICAL FAMILIES

From the creators of the life-changing series *Focus on the Family's The Truth Project®* comes a stunning new journey of discovery that explores family as a revelation of God—and the extraordinary impact families have on the world around them. Introducing *The Family Project™*, a transformative, feature-length documentary and DVD curriculum that reveals—through an in-depth exploration of God's design and purpose—biblical truths about the role of families in society.

The Family project™

A Divine Reflection

WE NEED YOUR HELP

STRONG FAMILIES ARE WHERE SO MANY OF OUR SOCIETY'S PROBLEMS WILL BEGIN TO HEAL.

Amidst the tragedy of divorce, fatherlessness and family brokenness, we can still have hope—hope that comes from the Gospel and from God's blueprint for the family. We need to lean into that hope, not away from it. And that's why I'm so excited about *The Family Project*—it will enable people around the globe to better understand the Creator's design.

At this pivotal moment, we need committed partners to come alongside us with their prayers and financial support. Please consider supporting *The Family Project*.

Jim Daly
President of Focus on the Family

VISIT
FamilyProject.com
TO LEARN MORE